Ballads of a Bred Souljah

JEFFREY BROWN

authorHOUSE®

AuthorHouse™
1663 Liberty Drive
Bloomington, IN 47403
www.authorhouse.com
Phone: 1-800-839-8640

First published by AuthorHouse   5/12/2010

ISBN: 978-1-4490-0102-5 (sc)

Printed in the United States of America
Bloomington, Indiana
This book is printed on acid-free paper.

Lost SoulJabz ©

I would like to thank everyone who has Contributed to the making, editing, financing, inspiration love... of this fine work I humbly show my appreciation to you all... So many to name, so very many so I say:

Amen.

This Book is Dedicated to Unconditional Love
— God, Family & Friends.

Dear Mama

4Mama

Why do u love me so
It hurts me
I know it pains u
None of my dreams have came true
I never blame u
Your nightmares seem reality
I pray that you're not mad at me
My current state is so sad to see
Ruined everything you've had 4 me
Waitin'
As if I swayed in the winds of satan
Defiled your creation
But I have no choice but 2 live
Only pray that you may 4give my short comingz
Hopefully better dayz r comin'
Ain't life somethin'
Certainly not a bed of roses
Now I know this
But I'm not hopeless
I got a love letter in my heart
And the Lord wrote it...

I apologize

I apologize
For the wet eyes
The lies
The dark skies
Lost smiles
Stress
Mess
Everything
Left
All that I couldn't and wouldn't do
Every bad thing I've ever done to you
Or anyone else
All the try 'n' fails
Puttin' you through hale
All the times I bailed
Wouldn't do what I was supposed to do
Afraid of disappointin' you
And Him too
Life ain't so simple
Tha flames kindle
My eyes twinkle
Twinkle twinkle

Ur Pain Iz mine

your pain is mine
That's Y I'm havin such a hard time
My demonz got step brothas
They're my motha's
I've adopted
Heard them plannin' murdah 'n' I couldn't stop it
That's Y I copped it
Not to kill or shop lift
It's tha Lord's gift
End tha war swift
Her tears are as potent liquor on my fresh sores
They burn…
But I can't seem 2 learn
How 2 seperate us
Her pain is in my vein
I'm her chil'
That's Y u ain't seen me smile in a while
Screamin' "make this all stop" her stress piles
2 my very las' breath chil'
I'm lovin' Mama Double Ves' style…

It Ain't Fair"

It It ain't fair that I am here

'N' you out there...

Despair

Fear

Your hands comb through the air

But I'm not near

Clasped in prayer

Pleadin' for His power

Every minute

Every hour

Held captive in this concrete tower

You toil the soil

Provide me with food that won't spoil

Light the oil

Adding sweet fragrance to your supplications

Your soul bless to have patience

Heart anticipates

Your fingers turn to Romans 8:28

And you meditate

To time or date,

I cannot relate

My days are repetitive

Yet they stagnate

I fight back the hate environment creates

A heavy weight

Bitter taste

Treated less than second rate

I labeled an inmate

But what I can't take

Is how my current state makes your heart ache

Increases my heart rate

It's hard to contemplate how I cannot control my fate

In here

You there

Wishin' I could make disappear

All the pain, fear, despair

It ain't fair

The Price

You've sacrificed so much
I can not give up
Or disappoint
So for we've come to reach this point
No blame-shall-I-point
It is my responsibility
To give you stability
After all that you've given me
My life could be so differently ...
Lived
So I thank you for every-thing-you-did
The long hours 'n' stress
Giving more than your best
With no rest
All the worry 'n' fret
'Till it pain your chest
(Oh how much I regret)
Yet you never falter or fail
To come to my rescue
You kept me next to ...
Correct that remark,
I've been IN your heart from the very start
We share the mark
When they say see me,
There you are
Many features the same

For from you I came
I take the loss if you shall gain
Since I know your pain
I shall never lose again
But I will do all I can
To be a stand up Man
Do all that I can with this life
Nothing less shall suffice
For you have paid the price
Of Sacrifice

Blame Me

Don't be so hard on yourself
The fault isn't yours... it can-not-be
BLAME ME...
See in' your hurt pains me
I want to break your chains free
That you may be whatever wherever you choose
I will take every single lash & bruise intended 4 you
See in' how my trails & tribulations claim you
I would take my portion times two
'N' sign my happiness over to you
For all the times your unconditional love came through
Throughout time you've made my skies blue
And all the treacherous nights too
No love in all creation is the same to me
My worst fear is you ever to be
Ashamed of me
If any fault or failure be,
Give the blame to me
Her pain, breathe
Her many tears, bleed
I cannot stay, down,
I must succeed.
There is no other choice 4 me
The lord's is the only voice I see
And so it shall be
As I SoulJah E-ter-na-lly

Let the flames of hell burn my feet
That the Gates of Heaven you may see
Finally free
BLAME ME…

"Mother Nature"

Dear mother of mine

Possessor of my sunshine

Banish the dark shadows every time they overtake my mind

For my sake you bind...

Demons 'n' Devils

Indeed, evils of every kind

You're so very fine

Refined by time

Your very face shines

Radiates from the unconditional love behind

And may I remind;

I love to fee your winds

Give flight to my broken winds

Help to sooth my broken limbs

It carries to you my spoken hymns

To you the birds shall sing

Only praising words I bring

To you...

A gain...

Your rain

Washes away the pain

And every stain that I have gained in vain

You quench the thirst of my frame to ease my strain

My fruits I dare not solely claim

For although I toil

You are the soil –

Proven loyal
To my seeds
Taking the blood I bleed
And every tear which escape from me
Indeed,
You are the Tree
Which shelters me
And offers Free…
The precious fruits of Thee
As I rest on the…
Strong roots I see
So Devine is Dear mother of mine

Fruits of Thy Labor

Brotha' of Min

Brother of mine

Our fates intertwine

But by 2 different designs

A different state of mind

One ready to erupt without a sign

I tend to take my time to shine as I mind my grin'd

Walkin' the very thin line as I climb

His heart is fortified

You'd never dream that he ever cried

This melancholy pride inside, I dare not deny

My water well runs dry behind my eyes

A lesson; you never learned yours;

You always had love for them whores!

I implore, you 2 speak no more

He believed all women walked on all fours

'Cept that mother of yours

Ours!!!

No chocolate or flowers

Every relationship he's soured

Every Conquest…

Devoured!!!

And I am still laughin…

I tend to be of another fashion

Although I can not dispute

Some are pros-ti-tutes!!!

Mute!

I know there are still many without Pollutes,

'N' strong Roots

Something did I for get ?

Oh, Yes!

I wear "SoulJah" on my shouldah

And he's a cloudy vapor

Hater!

Do me a favor...

Keep that!

I'll stay the "Player"

Alright Neighbor...

SeanShine

My newborn baby brother
There can be no other
To replace you
Within my heart
A special place I place you
Ever since you came into my sight
You've breathed a new breath into my life
Around you I'm never lonely
My lil' homie
A baby Souljah
Give u the best of me
If I could I would ensure your destiny
Ride with the Lord and you'll have no enemy
Let you know I appreciate the love you send to me
Baby boy brave and bold
Doesn't matter who your daddy is
All that matters is we family
Don't want you to ever be mad at me
Live a life of love gladly (radically)
Sean-there is no other
With love from your Souljah Big Brother

"Shayne"

You're so very tough
Mr. Little Stuff
Indeed;
More than jus a lil' rough
That's Y I love you so much
You swear you got Gorilla
OH! Don't cuss-
Guts!!!
Up for any task you're asked…
You refuse to be last
Not afraid to crash…
"Mr. Daredevil"
Baby Rebel
Unchained
And your love's the same
Untamed
Unchanged
Even when you call my name
Whether to ease your pain
Or play a video game
So very glad that from Heaven You Came
My life could never the same
Without Shane

"Hidden Blessings"

Dedicated 2 my sisters

Your prayers find me whenever I'm stressin or losin direction

Some times the state of my life seems depressin'

But your love never lessens

For it is without condition

So many years I'm missin' of the lives you're livin'

The many talents you're given…

I have not witnessed

That thought brings distress in the depth of my chest

You are the Flesh of my Flesh

The same Blood we Bleed

Yet we breathe so dis-tant-ly

Why must this be ?

Or is it me

Who speaks hypocricy

Did I never stop to see

That you were missin' me

Wishin' we

Could fulfill the words I promised thee

How can it be

That you cannot be

So very mad at me

My life changes so dramatically

So many things distracted me

Yet that is no reason

Just an explanation for the apparent Procrastination

Kin of the very same nation
Although estranged,
Brought forth by the same relation
Thus, No separation…
Nor space or distance
Can dismiss
The Love inherited in-this
My Truest wish
Is to be with
My Hidden Blessins'

I lye As

I lye as…
An innocent seed
Born into a world where my brothas bleed
Try to succeed but only fall on my knees
I lye as...
A new born
Child to those scorned yet celebrated
Born to be playa hated
Motivated
4 years I would have waited
See momma's smile glad her son's made it
I lye as…
A young Souljah in trainin'
Waitin' 4 it 2 stop rainin'
Strainin'
Body, mind and soul in engagin'
I lye as…what I die as

"Possibility"

The further time goes by
The more I wonder so very high
The question lingers so very high
Out of my reach
Although I may seek...
It's forever hurtin' me
Your pater-ni-ty
Every day lost is another eternity
That I'm wastin' nervously
If you are indeed one of my God-given Children
The love I've been given has been so long missin'
Those few moments we shared
I more than knew,
I FELT you cared!
And it hurts that I'm not there
Wherever that you might be
"Why has thou spite me"?
(2dead in the womb)
(2born in a tomb)
And one that might be...
The thought fright me
So my mind avoids-ever so slightly!
Even so,
Nightly!,
It might be,
The very thing which incites me

To persevere…
To where…
We'll both be made aware
And lay to rest the fear
Or should I even care?
Wherever you are, you might be happy there…
And it would not be fair
If I disturbed your reality
Your tranquility…
But it's killin' me!!!
When I consider The…
Possibility…

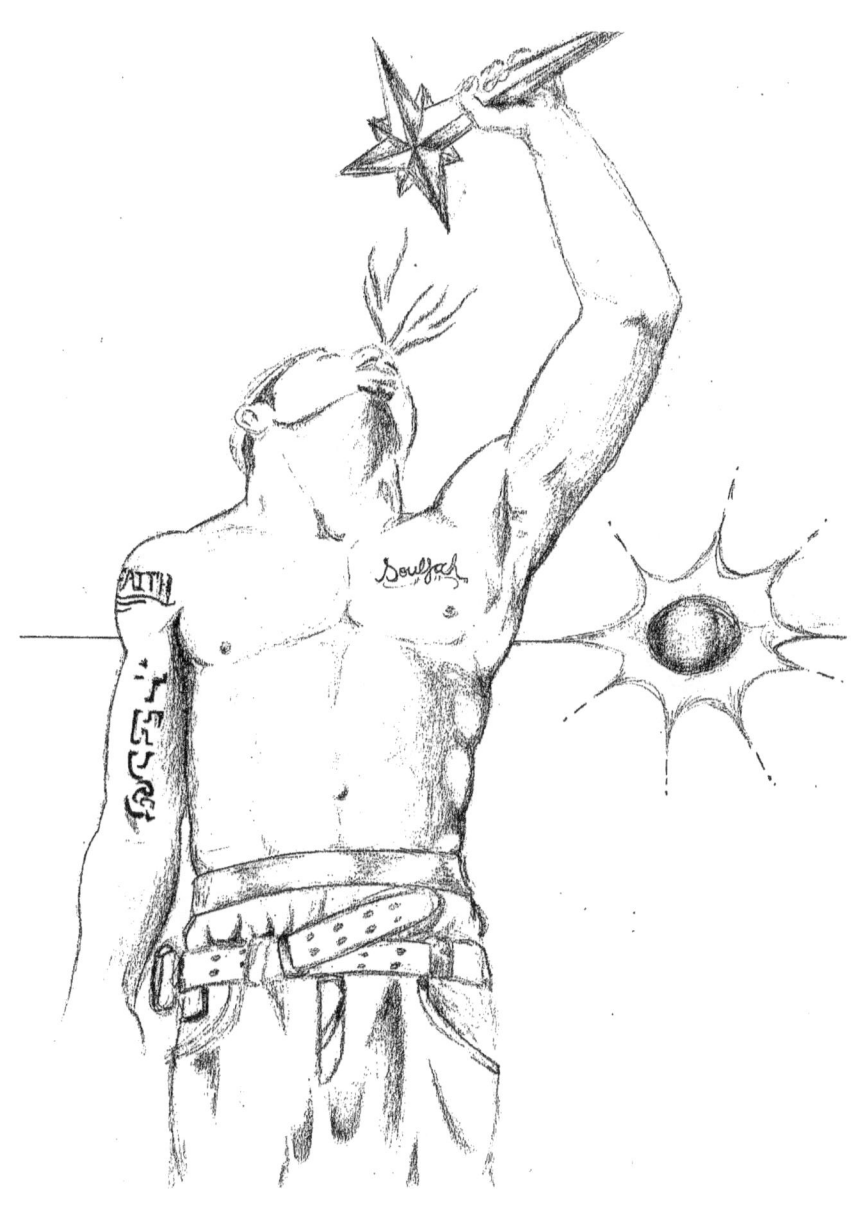

Borne

I Am

Souljah...
My destiny
Give y'all the best of me
Never selfishly
Souljah...
What I'm strivin' for
Ridin' for
Survivin' for
Souljah...
What I'm meant to be
My ancestors have sent to me
My inner entity
Souljah...
God's breath in me
Devilz testin' me
My angel ridin next to me
Got the world vexed with me
Souljah...
You hear me loud and clear
If-not-, come here
Let me yell it in your ear.
I'M A SOULJAH.

＊

My Vision

My vision of my mission
Is what I'm dishin'
Let your eyes consume
And your mind digest
First of all is my crest
The 9 pointed stars
It's depths are far
A shelter in peace
A shield in war
The 3 digits hall not diminish
Together they bear witness
To organizes self-expression that endless
Through vast mediums in the spirit of self dependence
Counteract the senseless
Which rapes weak defenses of those who don't sense it
Ignorant to terms such as knowledge of self
Spiritual health, generational wealth
And so much else
Either it's too boring"
Or just "foreign"
If sharing my personal scarring
Life experiences
Can make a difference
Or sharing my artistic ability
Can sharpen their minds visibility
Or maybe lyrically

I may share what makes sense to me
All in the hopes that eventually
A seed which is sent from me
May take root and profit thee
To some degree
Or in the very least
I may rest in Peace
Leaving a legacy to those who cherish me
Myself I share with thee though with you I may not be currently
Though some may not remember me
This is the... vision he... sent to me

4 My Sistahz

Where my Sistahs
Tha ones that know exactly where their gift's at
A loving heart and strong stance taking no smack
Down for whatever
'Cause whatever's clever 2 make things better
Nobody 2 impress, but her 'fit's tha best
No matter the size or duration, it's always good sex
No need for Mr.
She rather cash her own check
So much respec'
Ready 2 throw it down to the groun'
Never let it go
Quick 2 let you know…
"Don't call me Hoe"
'N' u bes' not forget it
Always by her Man's side, never behind
No time for tha ga'bage
2 Black Jesus, pay homage
'Cause he's my home
With my Sistah, this Souljah's never alone

Jewelz

My philosophy is my foundation
Bring my trinity into one nation
Focus the concentration
-Strive for positive
Elimination of Satan
Never forget the race 'n'
Keep pacin'
Don't hear their words
Ignore the playa hatin'
(keep on keepin' on)
Straight motivatin'
Forget livin' each day as the last
'cause what you just read is in the past
You'll always fall down
An endless battle
The eternal clash
'hood and evil
Good and the people
Can't feel how we do
Stay true
Ooohhhwwoooo let me ride w/ you…

7 Wondaz

When I unleash the mentals
My whole body trembles
Words explode through my dentals
Rapid erratic speech
Yet my neck still can't compete
Nor can my neck stay calm
As the venom spits,
It strikes like a Python
I might warn
That my hands cannot keep still
Swift as a Judo warrior,
They strike @ will
Neither are my legs patient
Vibratin' so hard that they shake the pavement
Pure Amazement...

I Carry On

The zest is missin'
What's this test I'm given
Never-the-less I'm livin'...
My life non-stop
Not even by writer's block
Can't-stop wont-stop 2 watch the clock
Though every second's precious
I pray that the Lord may bless us
All!
I must stand tall
Through all that I befall
I and I
Speak to Jesus and await his reply
My motha won't cry...
In vain
This pain shall not conquer
I stand longer
Endure... to be made stronger
And Overcome
His Chosen Son
Thy will Be Done
I ain't done...

"Focus"

Focus-

Enough of over stressin' and vexin' Thoughts perplexin'

Staggerin' steps unsure of directions

Can't let the winds of life choke us

Provoke us to fee hope's Crush to dust

Focus-

Don't fear the imagined evidence of the Pestilence

It doesn't make sense to flinch

Souljah is my essence

Ever since…

The Darkness was broke by the Word He has Spoken-2-us!

Focus-

"Stay focus beyond your plights"

Eternal Battle

"Me"

Look what serendipity's did 2 me
Wrong place, wrong time
But, Just Couldn't see what awaited me
Please Lord take these demonz away from me
They seem to be; Not afraid of me
But I scare me so easily
How does it feel 2 be… Your own worst enemy?
-I envy me-
Such a strong-willed entity
Through all the traits 'n' tribulations sent to me
A SoulJah! essentially…
-Oh how weak is me?-
Make the same mistakes repeatedly
His heart conquers the mind so easily
Like a sheep is he
Not knowin' where to go or where he needs to be
He doesn't even notice me … "oh woe is me"
And who is we-or should I say "me"?
I'm in the shadows so deeply
He doesn't even know he needs me
But all the while he feels me
All the pain 'n' negativity…This, he feeds me
When he's cut or crushed, he bleeds <u>Me!</u>
-<u>needs me…</u>-
to do what he can't do freely
like Slap a punk or cuss a ***** out easy!

But we deceive me
Locked back up Just as quick as we freed me
Now we sit face2 face and I ask if He remembers me
"Did your inner Child ever mention me?"
How he sent me free..?
When the world wouldn't Just let him be...?
Can't you see I'm your destiny?
This pompous prick is rexin' me!!!
Startin' at The Light that I dare not see!
Dear Lord
Please Enter Me...
Sippin' on this Hennessey w/ my worst En-emy...

"Take Care"

I try 2 care
But then I realize that no one hears the screams of my tears
Or sees my night marez
As my soul's light dwindles
Livin' this life is so far from simple
Circumstances more than coincidental
The anger surges
As the pattern emerges
Tempted then smitten
Kissed the bitten
And my heart's paid such a great price
Torn like Christ
this is My passion!!!
Tortured & tormented in the worst fashion
Im askin'...
Should I Just be heartless?
Tired of this "feelin' like a mark" mess
If my heart's brick-frozen,
How then shall it be broken?
Forget all the hopin' of elopin' with some women "Chosen"
All I see is hoes 'n'...
Lost little girls
Such a corrupted worl'
'N' I be a witness to this
So tempted to end it, (fed up wit' this)
With a flip of my wirst

And the pull of tha trigga
Death of anotha heartbroken sinner
(Wish I had never spoken wit' Her)
-Why do I even botha-
But I can't do that to my motha
I gotta go harder
Immortal martyr
Eternal Souljah
Gotta be my own shoulda
Though I'm well aware of the devil's stare (There)
Stripped bare
I must care even if no one's near...

"I Woke Up Screamin'...."

I woke up

Not wantin' to live

Or give

*A m***** $****

Dear Lord,

Please 4give my lips

But I must keep it real

Reveal how I feel with up most zeal

How can I deal...

With the trailz and tribulationz I'm facin'?

On a daily basis-

Open cases it amazes

How this system is so care-less

Never the Less

I do not fear this

Stand fearless

The fierces'

Fnail pitbull

-So don't come near this

As I share this

Burden burnin'

My inner yearnin'

Life's lesson,

Guess I'm still learnin'

Discernin' what the spirit's concernin'

-Its all there-

-Spiritual warfare-
No longer searchin'
I Feel you ℝ there!!!
So I have no fear
Of the ever present Pestilence
Nor any weapon formed against…
I still Repent
For They shall not relent
But The devils hurt to see
That they Cannot murder me
I SoulJah Eternally-

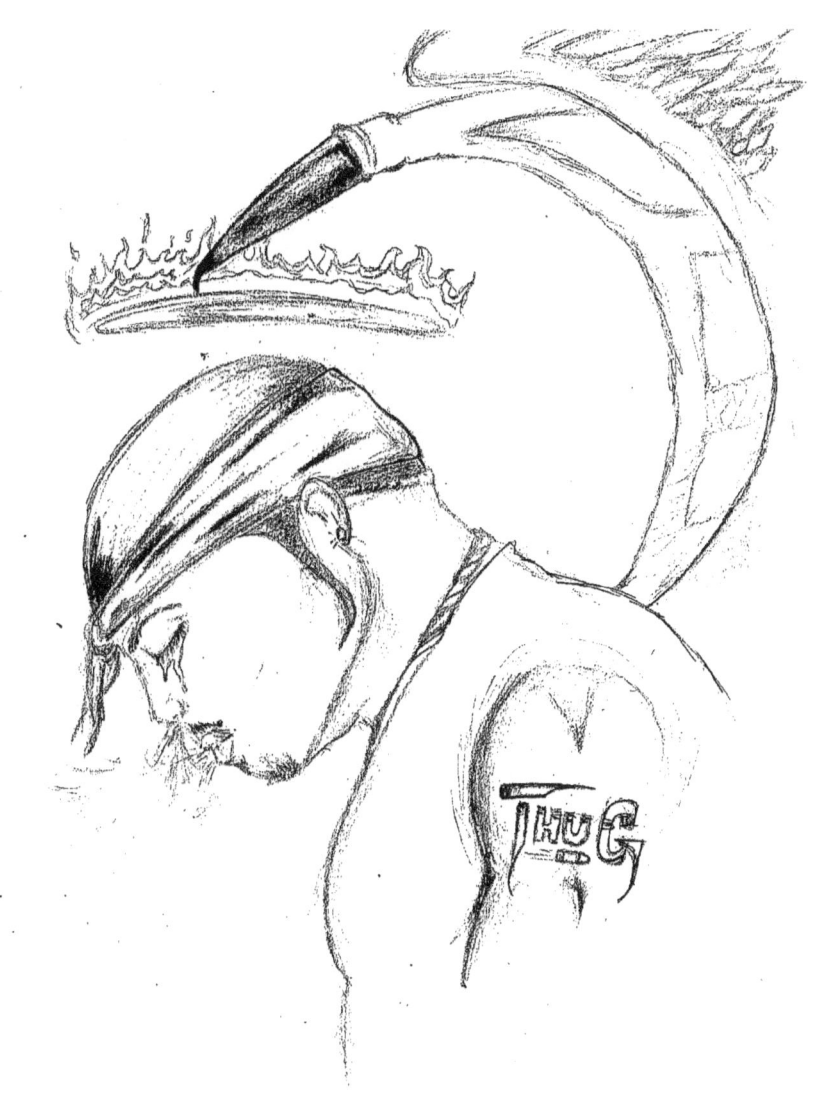

Duality

Tha Lesson

Tha lesson is…
Stressin' is…
In the atmosphere
All over here
And then you inhale (impale)
The demonz raze hell
Can't be seen
And has no smell
Corruptin' your thoughts
Misleadin' your memories
Make close friends out to be hated enemies
Always in the air
Always in your ear
Tellin' you "don't care"
Everyday everywhere
Make you cold stare
Life with no cheer
Like sittin' with no chair
Fallin' through the air
'til you're no longer here
all the time unaware>there're Demons in the air.

7

Dear Lord
Who art thou
Tell me how
I order you
I'm bored of you
Playin tricks on my head
Go 'head
And send me 2 Hell
And I'll land where I stand
This is my lan'
Inherited by my slave han'
So we're damned?
Who's savin' me
-Civil War-
Tha genesis of mental slavery
It's hypocritical
My lyrical is mythical
Or mystical
Pistol pulled
7 times
Bombarded by 7 rhymes 7 hunned and 77 timez

Nomesane

Brotherly love
I can't get enough
I don't get any
'cept for that little child in my dome
Prayin' to go home
Smokin' on a bone
Ready to grip the chrome
Grinnin'
But he's never winnin'-⊠sinnin'
Always lozin'
Surrounded by confusion, delusion trapped in seclusion
Goin' insane
But still maintain
Break the chain
And withstand the pain
Notin' to lose
Nothin' to gain
Hide the tears in the rain
Evrybody left
Are you stayin'?
Nomesane...

Bi-Design

The light there's uncertain

Inside I'm hurtin'

These thoughts so unnervin

Cryin...

The Lord to save me

His baby

Is she mine?

What is the Design Devine...

4 this life of mine?

I'm tryin'

But I fell

A mental hale...

Of troubling thoughts

That's brought

Such a cold heart

Torn apart

From the sinnin'

The flame is winnin' (I must keep The Fire)

My inner Children (my heart's desire

I inhale the smoke to choke the Demonz which Cloud my min'

As I walk this path of mine... such a thin line

A Bastard I'm...

Farther-less

Seed of the Martyr's Lus'

The Lord is a part of Us

As the Devils discuss the ways of the unjus'

How dare they Judge Us
Jesus!!!
I plead "Don't let US be crush"
I love you so much…
And I owe you much more
How much more shall you endure
Witness the pain of my sores
My soul endures
Implores the Lord to heal yours
Dear mother of mine
Unconditional love Devine
From this Heart of mine – By Design

2-Passionate

Until

I love
Fantasizing' your beautiful skin tone
Wishing' u were home alone...
Every day
So we may play
Mold together like clay
With you
In you
Clothes peeling'
Revealing
A beauty so appealing'
Lookin' from head to toe
I want u so...
Love it nice and slow...
You feelin' it grow
I'm feelin' it flow
It's so deep though
Only Lord knows
My love grows, flows unopposed
'Til the doors of time close and the eternal flame froze

Ur Touch

I want your touch
Do u feel my lust?
Feel ur body 'n' let the blood rush
I want u so much
Your brown skin-tone covering mine
My fingers trail down ur spine
Now ur plush ass is mine
Touch ur peak every time
-I slide in
Thrustin' deeper and deeper
-Trust me, I need her
Do whatever to please her
Get on my knees and tease her
-Make her cumm
Never let her go
Anywhere but ecstasy
As long as her body lye's next to me
The Lord has "Blessed" me
She fulfills me
-and none shall lessen me
So don't question me
When I say I'm in love
'Cause my baby's loving' me

Devine Obsession

Interaction
Sexual satisfaction
Forever lastin'
Layin' in the mist
As we kiss
What is this?
I'm smilin'
Open the doors of life and slide in
Stridin'
Our bodies become one
Under the sun
I feel it in the heart of me
You're a part of me
And I'm a part of you
My boo
Too good to be true
You more
Never less than
Divine Obsession

Flirtin'

Flirtin'
Tear the skirt 'n'
Get tha workin'
Tongue kissin'
Flippin' every position
-Listen-
Sweet hips
Tantalizin' hips
Lifted off every kiss
I miss this
Get blessed
As we caress
Chest 2 chest
Nothing less
I feel ur breath
Heat my neck
'Cause I'm about to catch wreck
Time 4 action
Passion
Physical satisfaction
Passion...

Oooohhh

Took my love away one day
Took my breath the next
Much more than sex
Without the latex
Yet so un-complex
So many stress
'specially me
in this darkness through which I can't see
lyes my Black Beauty
full nudity
late night and early mornin'
my fingers start explorin'
legs seperatin'
third leg elevatin'
matin'
love makin'
mixed with passion
lickin', stickin' and remeniscin'
my Baby Boo
ooooooohhhh, oooohhhhhh!!!
I love you too

I Meet...

I meet your body heat
In between my sheets
Split your feet
Get right beneath
Your belly button
Struttin' your hips
To the left
The right
All night
Layin' in my arms
Restin' easy
I'll make you feel me
Deeply
You say you need me
And I need you
2
together become one
under or above the sun
you are my loved one
oh, how deep my love runs
how deep my love runs

Xplicit

I miss the sex...
Your legs around my neck
My feet by your shoulders
Get my tongue out, it's over
Do it over and over
From your lips to the bottom of your spine
Everything between is mine
And DAMN you're fine
In the moonlight you shine
Dip the peaches in the crème
But it's not a dream
A 2 a.m reality
Morning sexuality
Midnight sensuality
Slap your ass 'n' you ain't mad at me
Hittin' it sparatically
Bussin' nuts romantically
And you won't be mad at me
Sexuality
Sex reality
Sex my sanity

As We...

Behind the curtain

Flirtin'

Tongues touch as the blood rush

Hot lus'

It's you I seek

4 the flesh is weak

let our bodies speak

about to reach the peak

feel the sensation

vibration shakin' the nation

taste ya lips

as I rock ya hips

to sleep

this is sweet

taste you from the top of yo' head 2 the soles of your feet

never endin' 'til it's all complete

got me harder than concrete

expect the bes'

nothin' less

sweat

as we sex

Matters of the Heart

A letter 4 my love...

A letter from my love
Like a dove from above
Milky chocolate word
Love the taste and I can't get enough
In this life that's rough
Your breath keeps me from getting' crushed
I love you so much
Though life ain't easy
I'll struggle 2 please thee
Take it easy
Please be...
Whatever you want to be
Your love is warmin' me
In this icy cold
Your beauty I behold
One day I'll be old
And I know you'll be right there
Ridin'
Right next to my wheelchair

U-2-Me

It's a definite
Not a maybe
I miss my baby
No matter how hard the day be
I gotta be harder
I wanna be your baby's father
You to be the aunt to my brother
Heal the wounds of your mother
By my side I can see no other
So why bother
To look
Every other Sistah gets shook
My baby beauty
A Rudy Cutie
Say your name as I feel on your booty
Tooty Fruity
But on the factual actuality
I just love your sensuality
Adore your sexuality
Love you emphatically
Because you care...

Secretz

Should I stay
Should I leave
I could not conceive
This happenin'
Wall against my back again
Do I lose either way?
No matter what I say?
How do I do what I'm going to
It's a 2-way street
But where should we meet?
Our love
You want nobody 2 see it
Such a painful secret
I can't believe it
Heard, but I didn't see it
Comin'
Am I forever runnin'...?
Into red lights
Cold nights
So many plights in this life

Digital Love

Lyrical dove
Chillin' with my digital love
Grab my Mickey
'N' send quickly
If you ever need me
Come 'n' get me
Don't regret me
'N' don't forget me
Do whatever you let me
Get me
Wherever you want
The memories taunt
Met through a digital line
Never alone when we on the phone
Love lasting' 'til the world is gone
Come on
On my mind from dawn to dawn
Always on yo' side
'N' I'll never be gone
Don't fail me
Email me

The Burning Question

In my heart the fire's churning'
Burnin'
As I'm yearnin' for your tender touch
I love you so much
I can't get enough
Makes me blush
The world's cold
But I'm warm
In my baby's arms
Safe from harm
I stay calm
Not stressed
'Cause I'm blessed
As I rest on your chest
Love got me high like cess
What is this thing
Awaiting the diamond ring
My joy in a world of sadness
Gladness in this madness
My serenity
Look at what God's sent to me
Love of the century
That's how it feel
Is it real...
But is it real ?

Never learn

My mind's still on you
-So many try to push it off
Into the abyss
But I Dismiss
Love
This is His Gift
At leas' what I feel is
A need to be with you
So many things lead to you
I'm needin' you
When you're with me
I'm feelin' you
I smoke to cloud my min'
So the love I clearly see shine
Hazy:for now I'm blind
Feelin' so sad and worthless
Show the world my heart
But I'm nervous
They always try to hurt it
Sparked the flame and burnt it
Lesson taught but I haven't learned it

2-1

Two years of our lives
So many times inside
A few times you've cried
And so have I
Oh my
So deep so quick
Our baby traveled back in time
But only for a moment
Then I knew you're who I wanted
Pictures and pounds of papers piled peacefully
Colorful
Wonderful
I'm in love with you
The sky above
The ground under you
So fond of you
Wanna bond with you
In so many ways
Got me in a daze always
Yet afraid

Situations

Situation

Contemplation

Something unexpected happened

Didn't wanna start rappin'

I met you

Was about to walk

But couldn't help but to stop by and talk

Then I got open

Words started flowin'

'Bout to stop

I just kept on goin'

I left the door open

But you couldn't step in

Love as a weapon

I'm stressin'

Thought I learned my lesson

But I guess I didn't

Should've kept my feelings hidden

Now I'm trippin'

Slippin'

But she never listens

To what I'm missin'

Situations

Get Back..

Missin' my baby
My lady
The friend that saved me
No ifs or maybes
It's an actual fact
Can't wait 'til I get back
Without my heart
I'll have a heart attack
When she comes
My heart's back
And my heart's Black
Chocolate brown to be exact
2 plus years
Don't want to give it back
And still they say I can't have that
Now how's that?
I'd fall flat on my back
If she didn't come back
Cut a brotha some slack
To get some get back
Get back

Done Changed

Things have changed
No longer the same
But who's to blame
Is it you?
Is it me?
Who could it be?
Maybe it's just the way things seem to be
Look at you
Look at me
Is this how it's meant to be
Life of complexity vexin' me
Fantasies of you sexin' me mentally
What are we meant to be?
Livin' love romantically
Or separately?
But that's not the life I want to lead
I want you to be with me
But don't forget our baby
Reborn
As we carry on...

My Crime

My past has come back to more than haunt me
Wonderin' if you still want me
I've hurt you so
How much I love
You may not know
For doing you wrong was the first I showed
but I must pay for my crimes I suppose
No matter how far back they go
Your memories won't let them go
But you'd leave me though
I truly want this seed to grow
Wishin' I could turn back time
But I don't want to lose my min'
Feelin' as though the tears I've caused
Killed my sunshine
Now I've banished my soul
To a dark life so cold
Payin' for my crime
Prayin'/Payin' 'til my bones grow old

"Nitemare/U-Kno"

I reminisce on the love that we shared
Not knowin' it would become my nightmare
As I returned from Over There
The love had already begun 2 disappear
I had plans for it to flourish
-"Dear God this isn't fair!"-
To forget about the despair
That had you scared
I wasn't aware
Of how deep your heart was seared
By my lack of care
For an Angel that God dared to share
'My worst fear-
Had materialized before my very eyes
Retribution for all the lies
to this very day ,my heart cries
Through every season
No matter the rhyme or reason
I had Committed High treason
On my kneez 'n'...
Pleadin'
That I may be forgiven while I'm still livin'
(With a Godly wife n' children)
You know that I care
In my heart You're forever there
But how do I dare

Speak those words into the night air
Hopin' that you might share
In the depths of your heart Somewhere...
...Deep beneath the surface 'n' safe from bein' hurt again
Not to see the earth we're in
Maybe some place after then..?
Or not even there
Why even Care

"Delilah"

I thought my prayers had been answered

-Not knowin' that she was cancer

My heart took control

So very weary of the lonesome cold

She'd been through so much

So very rough - but smooth to the touch

I did not consider or remember

The drama-ridden Past that I had with her

I let it melt away with the winter of last December

All I was thinkin'

Was a new beggin'

Turn the pages

Didn't notice the sudden changes

Blinded by hopes

Didn't notice that my eyes were cloaked

Like the magician's smoke

-No mirrors

Caught-up in my own minds visions

Detached from reality

My life had changed drastically

-KLAP!!-

(It took that)

For my mind to come back

-Glad to be free

Now I want to go back and see ...

Devil's on my back tellin' me 2 get the "gat" &----Spree!

But it all went accordingly
To how it was meant to be (for me)
- A Tribulation that I was meant to see
Not to say it was "Happily.."..
Just to say He Carried me
Due to the fact I endured,
I Grew more... Souljah to the Core
All praises Be 2 the Lord
But this is my hearts Dream ....
This is my Soil's Nightmare...

"Forbidden Fruit"

I have yet to savior
Your once forbidden flavor
I can never forget how we first met
Or better yet,
I should said "first word read"
Now locked away at the foot of my head's love bed
-Sealed with a kiss-
In my situation
It was hard to keep patience
In my mind's awakened
It's so sad to say then...
That this relatin'
Would've had my life so easily taken
But that was back when...
Okay... I'm back again
You've become more than a friend
I don't really need them
So what are you to me then?
Not blood nor family
Yet you care for my sanity
You speak of "we" and "us"
How can someone I've never yet touched
Feel so much?
Yet I ...
Cannot deny
The rush between us

At first,

It seemed lust

Now in my dreams I've seen "us"

Shall I have what I've dream of ?

Forbidden Fruit

Destination U/K

Into the Depths

'bout to jump in
But I don't know the temperature
Ending the...
Long time of confusion
Walk in blind eyed
And the door closes behind me
"no turnin' back now"
-But there's no need to remind me
Livin' life lost you'll find me
If I pass through your life
Never mind me
Unless you truly love me
Hold
Don't just hug me
God don't like ugly
So He hates what I go through
I love
But I don't even know you
So much I got 2 show u
But you don't want to look
'til the day my life gets took

"The Plight"

I ain't been eating right
Can't sleep at night
Future doesn't seem that bright
This is what it's like
Plight of my life
As I fight to keep my sight
Of my Purpose…tempted to think it all worthless
So very nervous
As my fate contemplate
Awake in a wretched state
Inmate!….
Is what they label me
Enslaved legally
Freedom taken so easily
So easy to see…
It's all about the currency
"So what's the rate currently?"
200 for everyday they keep me away
So it's easy to say it's just a game that they play to get Paid
As our families Pray
And our sanity sways
But the whole world Pays when we can't contain the pent up rage
The strange fruit of their Unjust ways
(Singin' the same song from back on the Plan-ta-tion)
Penitentiary slaves of this New Age
A Hellish Generation

"A Place Call Home"

Cool breeze n' red dirt

The place of my birth

And where I shall rest in earth

It never gets cold

Place of my Ancestral Souls

Hill top rebels of old

So many stories told

Black Green and Gold

When I think of you,..

I feel invincible

My life's principles:

Foremost the spiritual

Don't be no fool

To thine own self be true

Work hard for you

It's strange

There's been so much change

Still

No other home I claim

"NYC"

New York City's still is mine
Q-Borough to put it simply
Sometimes I wonder where the days went
You taught me the rules of the pavement
Sometimes a hard pill to swallow
You were my mate role model
Shadow me footsteps to follow
While others were skirt chasin'
You gave me Foundation
The basic rules to not be swayed by fools
Taught me to keep my cool
Things I would never learn in school
Ciphers never stopped
Kich'n' Hip-Hop on Projec' rooftops
L.B Fam B.I.G and 2Pac
Prince Son is me
N.Y.C

"Comrades"

In close quarters daily
Thinkin' to myself
"Battle Buddy, please don't fail me
Pythonz strikin' daily
Livin' it up
No matter how the day be
My comrade
Has what I have
Is what I am
Gets me good when I'm bad
If he falls
We're both damned
Adopted Sons of Uncle Sam
BAM...
That's my cannon
Breakin' it up like Bruce Bannon
Seek shelter when u see the shell landin'
No use
You're not withstandin'
The spit I drop
And it just won't stop
Pythonz
Sinkin'/hittin' 'til we reach the top
And so on...
Spit shined 'n' creased
Our duty is to keep the peace

I would give my own
Before I let you lye deceased
The warrior's Ethos...
Is my belief
We slave together
Fit, shower 'n' shave together
Together we brave the worst weather
Front 'n' Center
I salute you
I couldn't do
Without you
Closer than a brother or sister
For our bond is thicker
If even severe
It shall not wither
From December to December
I shall always remember
My Comrades

Basic Training

Division is death
With every breath
Every time the groun' touchez my ches'
I wonder what's bes'
Life like the res'
Or this life of stress
½ a secon' 2 get up
Next half to drop
Between these,
At ease
But no time to breathe
Runnin' on 'E
I fall to my knees
Askin God please
Get me through these
Weeks
But how dare I speak
Knowin I need the discipline
Wonderin' who is listenin
Peace at night
Wake up-I'm here again…will it ever end

"Was it Worth it?"

What is the purpose
To be in the desert furnace
In a land where the people cursed us
Each with a desire to hurt us
Serving our country
As she desert us
Hopes crushed
And my soul's so nervous
Cry to God unsure if He heard us
I've committed so many murders
But it's not unheard of
It' common place in the place in this place we are placed
Tomorrow's so easily erased
I play it safe…
Locked-n-loaded-Just in case
Another tragedy must-take-place
I take the guilt
You take the crate

"Fallen Soldier"- Spc.Walters"

I take another breath
Taste the stress back of my throat
Back of my throat
To the depth of my chest
Wondein'
Why there's any breath lest
When so many lye breathless
In that place I lest
Where Death won't rest
Pain won't sleep
And troublin' thoughts won't cease
As you pray for peace
Beg and plead
Prayin' that you leave
Finally, orders received
By the momentary reprieve
A hard thing to learn
You've been called to return
To the bloody sounds that burn
Eager to turn...
Your Happy times with family
Into thoughts & dreams that tear at your sanity
How can this be?
That nothing happen to me
Left to live a life that's sad to see
I pray they're not mad at me

"Army of One"

I went where you told me to go

Do you not love me any more?

I did what you told me to do

Yet you say "I don't know you"

How could you?

After all these years

Blood, sweat and tears

You fed and clothe me

How dare you say that you don't know me

Were all those lies you told me

Dreams you sold me

Be All You Can Be

Land of the Free

But now I see

The only Army is me…and He

"War Vet"

The troubling thoughts I get

Cold sweat

Chemical balance upset

Mental misery

The foreign spirits that visit me

Remnants of Uncles Sam's killin' spree

All in the name of Liberty

But do you see

The finger on the trigger belonged to me

So how could I expect to be

Trouble free

But don't judge me

For you All agreed

When you saw the Towers bleed

Oh yes

We Shall Never Forget

Now I get no rest

Guess it's what we get

War Vet

Happy Home

A happy home...
It's been so long
And so hard to carry on
Seem like all my good days R gone
A part of me died in the war zone
My flesh didn't get touched
But I'm losin' my life 'n' my hopes R crushed
Left my mama's arms
'N' ran 2 his
But it was like I wasn't even one of his kids
Can u believe this...?
Went back 2 my motha's titty but the milk wasn't the same
But it was I who changed
Taste buds got used 2 malt liquor and green bud
Moved down 2 the A Town
All the negativity's away now
Oh wow...
Time 4 college
New peers
Check the dorm, I'm there
My worst fear
I was forced up outta there
If not there
Then where
Do I belong (do I fit in)
How could I be strong?

Journeys cut short

Cursed fate of some sort

It's hard 4 me 2 be all I can be..

Maybe the Army's wantin' me

Now I'm a war veteran

But I'm vexed again

This too has come to an en' my frien'

And then

Head back to the household

This life gets old

I'm so cold

Back home is stress and confusion

My delinquent brotha I'm losin'

-Why R u abusin'

My life

-This is my life…

'N' I'm so alone

'N' not knowin' where I roam

All I want is a Happy Home

Changed Man

"Everlastin'"

I hear you callin' me louder
But your voice falls faint
Not a full blown sinner,
But Lord, I am no saint
Seen so many efforts cut short in this lifetime
4 this life I'm…
Ever so grateful
For I know The Lord Perfects…
Whatever He makes you
For all that I go through
Through It all I'm glad that I know you
You Are by far such am amazing God
God Worthy to be praised all of my days
Days Turn to nights but I have no fright of word nor sight
Sight I shall not lose of the strength found in Christ
Christ To my right through all my plights 'n' fights
Fights And wars with Demons and devils
Devil Tremble at my feet for I walk in Peace
Piece By peace, I am perfected, not a crumb neglected
Neglected And scorned since the very day I was born
Born Into such a sinful world – the flesh
Flesh Less my soul's eternal, forever - everlastin'
Everlastin' Love, mercy and compassion
Compassion Underserved you heard every word, witnessed every deed
Deed Cannot gain me the name you've named me to be
Be A faithful servant is what I yearn for

For I do not want to do it on my own anymore
More Than I could possibly ask for you've had in store before
Before The very foundation you've known me most Passionate
Passion Yes! I feel you draw closer yet
Yet I repent
Lord, Shower me with your Love
Please Do Not Relent
Jeffrey B
Souljah Ent.

Life...For The Love

I look at life
And it ignores my gaze
Maybe she doesn't like my ways
If she look back
I wonder what I may say
To sway
Her to see things my way
Convinced to play
Enjoy every sun ray
Although some may say...
"Life is not to be lived that way"
They prefer to stay
Decay
Under dark skies dismayed
What a cold shoulder life displayed
-Suffer as you grow older
-Then it's over
To say
That one day
This was the way I stayed
Led astray by my own melancholy ways
Gazed fixed to the grave
As the other children played
In solitary I stayed
My short lived childhood days
Even when I put aside childish ways

Life still behaved...
Like a virgin maid
Who only stayed to evade...
Any advances made
Never to be tamed by my most intricate plans made
The one day with clasped hand I prayed
Not mine, but His way
In my ear I hear soft lips say...
"With you I shall forever stay"

Take A Knee

I kneel at the foot of the cross
This End of Day
Not only to pray
Or display my heart's dismay
As my eyes lay
Upon such a price you've paid
That all of my days be saved
From damnation of devilish ways
Never before did I envision
So much of your flesh missin'
From Barbaric incisions
The non-stop rippin's from whippins...
Done to thee
It pain me to see
The many pains you took for me
So how dare it to be
I let this world defeat me
I owe so much more to thee
For before I come to be,
You life you gave for me
So without hesitation
I give you my dedication
This word that's come to me
Shall not return vacant
My love is long suffering and patient
Just as the love you have for me

As a noble Souljah,
I take a knee
You've made me free
By the blood you bleed
-Head bowed and eyes closed-
But now I see
My gain by your loss
As I kneel at the foot of your cross
I cry in awe of Thee...

Father/Son Time

He stood there
At the edge of the sidewalk
Facing opposing streams of red & white lights
And when it ceased
He paced across the street as if led by foreign feet
When the other side was reached
The words paved between his teeth
Parted his lips
Darted through drips
Without fore warnin'
His soul's outpourin'
Marchin' a thin margin'
Bright white lights chargin'
He maintained sight of them
On the side of him
He kept walkin'
Lyrically talkin'
Only pausin'
For His silent response
Then the words resumed
Thoughts fears, questions & reflections
Passionately punctuated by physical statements
Arms at war with the elements
To counter-balance the verbal eloquence
No idea of where his words shall take him
The flow of thoughts still racing as he reaches the destination

Takes two steps with patience
Now safe from...
The Demons which chased him
His eyelids down
Lips without sound
Knees bound upon Holy ground
It rest under the Church Crest
The Cross
His thoughts not lost
He does indeed listen
The father Loves His Children
None shall be missing - (A Family Called Christian)